MW00884658

This Journal Belongs To:

Journals to write in

Positive Party Publishing
SUGAR LAND, TEXAS

Made in the USA
Monee, IL
06 October 2021

79514351R00068